D1175882

ENGINEERING SUPER STRUCTURES

ROADS

PAIGE V. POLINSKY

Consulting Editor, Diane Craig, M.A./Reading Specialist

Sandcastle

An Imprint of Abdo Publishing
abdopublishing.com

abdopublishing.com

Published by Abdo Publishing, a division of ABDO, PO Box 398166, Minneapolis, Minnesota 55439. Copyright © 2018 by Abdo Consulting Group, Inc. International copyrights reserved in all countries. No part of this book may be reproduced in any form without written permission from the publisher. SandCastle™ is a trademark and logo of Abdo Publishing.

Printed in the United States of America, North Mankato, Minnesota

062017
092017

THIS BOOK CONTAINS
RECYCLED MATERIALS

Design: Kelly Doudna, Mighty Media, Inc.
Production: Mighty Media, Inc.
Editor: Rebecca Felix
Cover Photographs: Mighty Media, Inc.; Shutterstock
Interior Photographs: Federal Highway Administration, iStockphoto, Library of Congress, Shutterstock

Publisher's Cataloging-in-Publication Data

Names: Polinsky, Paige V., author.
Title: Roads / by Paige V. Polinsky.
Description: Minneapolis, MN : Abdo Publishing, 2018. | Series: Engineering super structures.
Identifiers: LCCN 2016962883 | ISBN 9781532111044 (lib. bdg.) | ISBN 9781680788891 (ebook)
Subjects: LCSH: Roads--Juvenile literature. | Roads--Design and construction-- Juvenile literature. | Civil engineering--Juvenile literature.
Classification: DDC 624--dc23
LC record available at http://lccn.loc.gov/2016962883

SandCastle™ Level: Fluent

SandCastle™ books are created by a team of professional educators, reading specialists, and content developers around five essential components—phonemic awareness, phonics, vocabulary, text comprehension, and fluency—to assist young readers as they develop reading skills and strategies and increase their general knowledge. All books are written, reviewed, and leveled for guided reading, early reading intervention, and Accelerated Reader™ programs for use in shared, guided, and independent reading and writing activities to support a balanced approach to literacy instruction. The SandCastle™ series has four levels that correspond to early literacy development. The levels are provided to help teachers and parents select appropriate books for young readers.

EMERGING • BEGINNING • TRANSITIONAL • FLUENT

CONTENTS

About Roads

Roads are hard, flat surfaces.

They help people travel from one place to another.

People first built roads
6,000 years ago.

They used
timber
and stone.

Roads gave people smoother, faster paths to follow. People safely carried goods on roads.

People also used carts on roads.
This improved trade.

Today, people use cars and trucks on roads.

These **vehicles** are heavy. So roads need to be very strong.

Modern roads are made of **asphalt**
and **concrete**.

They connect towns, cities, and even countries!

US **Route** 66 is a famous road.
It passes through seven states.
It begins in Illinois.

It was one of
the first US
highways built.

Roads take a long time
to build. **Engineers** plan
carefully.

They create the best **routes** for travelers.

Builders make sure roads are smooth. Bumps and holes can **damage vehicles**. So can flooding.

Roads are sloped
to keep water
from pooling.

19

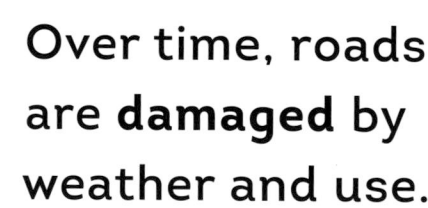

Over time, roads
are **damaged** by
weather and use.

Workers **repair** them. With proper care, roads can be used for centuries.

Think About It

Roads help you get to many places.
Where do you travel on roads?

GLOSSARY

asphalt – a black, tarlike substance that is mixed with sand and gravel.

concrete – a mixture of sand, gravel, cement, and water that becomes hard when it dries.

damage – to cause harm or ruin.

engineer – someone who is trained to design and build structures such as machines, cars, or roads.

highway - a major road, especially one that people use to go from one town to another.

repair – to fix something.

route – a road, path, or course that is followed to get from one place to another.

timber – cut wood used for building.

vehicle – a machine used to carry people or goods.

Weeks Public Library
Greenland, NH